Medical, Genetic & Behavioral Risk Factors of Great Danes

By: Ross D. Clark, DVM

H. DAVID HAYNES, DVM – LEAD RESEARCH
AND EDITORIAL ASSISTANT
ART J. QUINN, DVM, DACVO – PROFESSOR EMERITUS,
OKLAHOMA STATE UNIVERSITY CENTER
FOR VETERINARY HEALTH SCIENCES
BRAD HOWARD, DVM – RESEARCH ASSISTANT
PAUL SCHMITZ, DVM – TECHNICAL ASSISTANT
JAN COODY, MBA – TECHNICAL ASSISTANT
NITA RITSCHEL – EXECUTIVE ASSISTANT
GERI HIBBLEN JACKSON – PHOTO ACQUISITIONS
LINDA A. CLARK, RVT, AKC JUDGE – PHOTO ACQUISITIONS

To order additional copies of this book or other
breed books of the 179 AKC recognized breeds by
this author, contact: Xlibris LLC
1-888-795-4274
www.Xlibris.com Orders@Xlibris.com

Medical, Genetic & Behavioral Risk Factors of Great Danes

INSIDE:

BY: ROSS D. CLARK, DVM

PREFACE

This book provides you with a through description and positive attributes of this breed including origin, purpose, history, normal heights and weights, acceptable colors and behavioral traits. Our books differ from most books on dog breeds because this book also provides you with a comprehensive and authoritative source of all the known predisposed hereditary health syndromes for the breed. You will find extensive references for each problem described. We also provide the breed club address for this breed and a list of laboratories and organizations that can provide professional help and information.

Many genetic disorders are common to several breeds. We do not intend to convey severity of incidence by the length of text within a particular breed chapter. One breed may have forty percent incidence and another breed only four percent. If a thorough study has been done to indicate the percentage of incidence, we make note of it; however, please keep in mind the incidence is only an indicator of the dogs tested. A breed for instance may show eighteen percent incidence of hip dysplasia as indicated by OFA, although breeders and veterinarians may not elect to submit radiographs of hips so severely dysplastic that the owners and their veterinarians know that there is zero chance to be rated as OFA normal.

After developing a practice that catered to clients with show dogs, my interest in each breed continued to grow as I studied and observed more and more about the unique predisposition and incidence of health problems in each breed. Breeders of purebred dogs for show were a challenge and inspirational for me to research and help them with their unique health problems. Historically references to hereditary problems are scattered throughout various Veterinary medical texts and journals such as ophthalmology, neurology, gastroenterology, cardiovascular and dermatology. This book, as well as the other books and articles I have written, is researched and compiled with the intention to provide both veterinarians and dog owners with comprehensive and authoritative predisposition information under the breed name.

At the date of this publication, The American Kennel Club Canine Health Foundation and the The Kennel Club of England reports over 400 known hereditary health syndromes throughout the dog kingdom. At the writing of my first book in 1983, less than 50 hereditary issues are able to be predicted and or diagnosed. Sequencing of the canine genome, DNA tests, metabolic testing including blood tests and urine testing; plus, phenotypic examinations such as radiographs, ultrasound, and CERF or OFA eye registry exams by a Board Certified Veterinary Ophthalmologist have advanced the science of breed related health and behavioral problems.

This book will provide veterinarians, researchers, pet owners and breeders with a comprehensive guide to all the known problems veterinarians and dog owners should consider during pet selection and throughout each life stage of our canine friends.

NOTE

The fact that a breed shows many disorders may be more an indication of the extensive research done on that breed than on its comparative soundness of the breed.

Many genetic disorders are common to several breeds. We do not intend to convey severity of incidence by the length of text within a particular breed chapter. One breed may have forty percent incidence and another breed only four percent. If a thorough study has been done to indicate the percentage of incidence, we make note of it; however, please keep in mind the incidence is only an indicator of the dogs tested. A breed for instance may show eighteen percent incidence of hip dysplasia as indicated by OFA, although breeders and veterinarians may not elect to submit radiographs of hips so severely dysplastic that the owners and their veterinarians know that there is zero chance to be rated as OFA normal.

Please be aware that we have included and identified anecdotal information, defined by Merriam Webster's dictionary as unscientific observation; however, the observations of breeders and veterinarians with a special interest in the breed will hopefully be converted to scientific research, often underwritten by breed clubs, to confirm or rule out predisposition to breed problems.

You will note that each chapter is thoroughly referenced to help with the reader's research as well as to credit and appreciate the researchers, writers, and breeders that have helped the animal world and mankind by their work with these genetic disorders.

Ross D. Clark, D.V.M.

TABLE OF CONTENTS

x

GREAT DANE

Harlequin great dane

ORIGIN AND HISTORY

Magnificent size and supple grace characterize the "Apollo" of dogs—the Great Dane. Its origins are believed to be the Irish wolfhound and old English Mastiff. The dog of today has existed for over 400 years and was originally bred in Germany to run down and fight the wild boar. Sixteenth century etchings depict Great Danes hunting with great agility. In the 18th century one observer reported "No equipage can have arrived at the acme of grandeur until a couple of harlequin Danes precedes the pomp."

Today's gentle Dane remains an alert guard dog that conducts itself with tact even in small apartments.

DESCRIPTION

Stable, sweet temperament with proper training is most important in the Great Dane. Unusual temperament is caused by environment and training, physical conditions, and inheritance.

Brindle great dane

Fawn and brindle puppies look very dark at birth—almost black—but gradually change to the normal expected color within 3 to 5 weeks. The pink feet and nails turn black within the first week. Blue puppies are also darker at birth and the skin often looks blue when wet. Black puppies are born black. Excessive white on any puppy (other than Harlequin) is most objectionable. (See Great Dane disqualifications).[1] Harlequin puppies are white with irregular torn black patches. On Harlequins, the pink skin, feet and especially the nose turn black more slowly. The tiny black spots on the nose gradually enlarge and spread together at a time rate according to the number and size of spots. Harlequin color is very unpredictable and each individual varies. The color sometimes changes during the first year by developing more spots, ticking or by the patches growing larger and running together. The harlequin pattern is a result of interaction of the merle gene (PMEL17) and the harlequin gene (PSMB7) on black pigment. Harlequin pattern develops when a dog carrying the dominant merle gene inherits a copy of the harlequin gene. No dog has been found with two copies of the harlequin gene presuming that pairing is embryonic lethal. Mismarks (colors other than described in the Great Dane Standard) such as merles, solid white or predominantly white puppies are euthanized by many breeders, as they often carry lethal genes, deafness and many unforeseen problems that may develop. Vita Tech labs offers a DNA test for the merle pattern in dogs. The UC Davis Veterinary Genetics Lab offers a DNA test for the harlequin pattern. [38]

Rear dewclaws are most unusual but should be removed if present. Front dewclaw removal is optional. Do not dock tails-a crook in the tail is rare, but if present at birth, can sometimes be corrected by squeezing the tail and rolling it between the fingers until it is straight, then splinting with stiff tape.

Ear cropping is optional but desired by owners. Ears are cropped medium-long (4 to 5 inches from top of skull to top point of ear). This may look long but the head will grow into the size. The best time to crop is at 25 pounds, or 12 weeks, as size varies in litters. Cropping does NOT make ears stand. The postoperative care plus consistent taping (with or without frames) to support the ear is the answer to standing ears.

harlequin and mantle great danes running

THE SHOW RING

Great Danes[1] height must be at least 28 inches for bitches with the ideal being 30 inches or greater and 30 inches for dogs with the ideal being 32 inches or greater. Average age of maturity is 2 1/2 to 3 1/2 years. Usually the slower maturing Danes live longer. Average approximate weights for dogs are: small, 115 pounds; medium, 130 pounds; and large, 150 pounds. Weights for bitches are: small, 110 pounds; medium, 120 pounds; large, 130 pounds. There is no maximum limit on height or weight.

Disqualification faults include Danes under minimum height; any color other than those described under "Color, Markings, and Patterns"; docked tails and split noses.

BREEDING AND WHELPING

The normal Great Dane requires no special care during gestation other than good-quality food and exercise. Litter size averages eight to 10, with older bitches whelping slightly fewer in number. All bitches need close watching the first three days after whelping, as puppies are often suffocated by the bitch unknowingly lying on them. Birth weight ranges from 3/4 to 1 1/2 pounds. Large litters often need some supplemental feeding, using regular baby-size nipples and bottles. A standard commercial formula is the safest and best to use. Feed at 6- to 12-hour intervals, depending on need, leaving the puppies with the mother between times for cleaning, warmth and the natural need to nurse. Puppies will suck each other if unable to get to their mother.

blue great dane puppy

Weaning begins at 21 days or sooner if possible as Great Dane puppies usually have teeth by 3 weeks of age. Puppies should be weaned by 4 to 5 weeks.

GROWTH

The most rapid and stressful growing time is from 4 to 10 months. During this period the tendency to over dose with vitamins is most common. This often causes stress and improper nutritional balance that can lead to faulty assimilation and utilization of the food. A natural, well balanced, wholesome diet is the safest and best way to feed, although a high protein stress type of diet is sometimes necessary. Common stress signs caused by improper diet are splay feet, broken down or enlarged pasterns and hocks, dull dead coat, drooping ears, arching the back, pot bellies and excessive soft stools. Nutritional problems are best checked by doing a hair analysis and/or a blood calcium phosphorous ratio.

Photo by Lisa Jernigan Bain

14

RECOGNIZED RISK FACTORS
IN GREAT DANES

CARDIOVASCULAR-HEMATOLOGICAL-RESPIRATORY

VonWillebrands disease (VWD) [12 (265)] has been reported in the Great Dane. This refers to a deficiency of vonWillebrand's factor, a glycoprotein that when combined with Factor VIII, is responsible for platelet adhesion. Clinical signs include increased bleeding time after surgery or trauma.

Great Danes are at greater risk for **subaortic stenosis** [13, 15] and **persistent right aortic arch.** [12 (209)]

The Great Dane's heart is subject to both **mitral valve dysplasia** [14] and **tricuspid valve dysplasia.** [16a] The abnormally developed valves can have thickened valvular leaflets, underdeveloped papillary muscles and cordae tendineae. Regurgitation of blood into the atria is common to both conditions, but myocardial failure has been seen with mitral regurgitation in large dogs. [14] **Degenerative mitral valve disease** has also been reported in the Great Dane. [14]

Dilated cardiomyopathy (DCM) is the most significant heart disease in the Great Dane. The Dane is the third most common breed diagnosed with DCM. [14] Clinical signs include ventricular dilatation, congestive heart failure and atrial fibrillation. Pedigree analysis suggests that DCM in Great Danes may be inherited as an X-linked recessive trait. [17] Investigations that a defect in the gene producing dystrophin, a muscle protein, may be involved are ongoing. [15] Annual echocardiograms are recommended, especially for breeding stock.

Another myocardial disease reported in the Great Dane is **myocardial fibroelastosis.** [14] This is a rare condition characterized by focal thickening of the left atrium, ventricle and mitral valve.

Great Danes are one of the breeds reported to suffer from **idiopathic hemorrhagic pericardial effusion.** [13, 14] An inflammatory process appears to affect the pericardial blood vessels and lymphatics resulting in effusion. The affected dog usually presents with cardiac tamponade and right heart failure. **Primary lymphedema** [12, 18] has also been recognized in the rear limbs of young Great Danes.

The breed appears to be over-represented in the incidence of **Cryptococcus infections.** [13]

DERMATOLOGICAL

Merle patterning occurs in the Great Dane. While merle is not an acceptable color in the breed, they do occur. [15a] Merle pattern is characterized by patches of dilute pigment and is inherited as an incomplete dominant gene due to retrotransposition insertion in the SILV gene. [25] Heterozygous merle dogs are usually normal but homozygous merles may have multiple defects, most often deafness and ocular abnormalities. Harlequin Danes are heterozygous merle and light marked Harlequins are most always homozygous merle. A mutation in the harlequin gene (H) interacting with heterozygous merle gene is responsible for the harlequin pattern. A missense mutation in the B2 subunit of the PSMB7 gene is responsible for the harlequin pattern. A direct DNA test has been developed to determine which dogs carry the heterozygous and homozygous merle genes as well as the harlequin pattern. [26, 32, 38]

Color dilution alopecia has been reported in blue Great Danes. [12(768), 13] Hair loss begins dorsally and spreads to all dilute colored areas. Retinoids may be a useful treatment. [16b]

Epidermolysis bullosa is characterized by the formation of bullae on the oral mucosa, footpads and pinnae. In the Great Dane, collagen targeting auto-antibodies have been implicated. [12(793)]

Great Danes may be predisposed for **idiopathic sterile granuloma** and **pyogranuloma**. [18] Firm, non-pruritic plaques appear on the head and pinnae. Lesions may become ulcerated and secondarily infected, but respond to glucocorticoids.

Young Great Danes have a predilection for **demodicosis** [18] and a **zinc responsive dermatosis** [18] caused by feeding zinc deficient diets.

The unpigmented areas of the Harlequin Great Dane are at risk for **solar dermatosis** [18] and increased risk of **squamous cell carcinoma**.

Great Danes are predisposed for **acral lick dermatitis** [18] and pressure points are subject to **hygroma** and callus **formation**. Continued trauma to these areas can result in **callus dermatitis** and **pyoderma**. [18] The breed is also predisposed toward **muzzle folliculitis and furunculosis** [4, 18] and **pododermatitis**. [13]

Great Danes are one of the breeds predisposed for **histiocytomas**. [13, 18]

ENDOCRINE-EXOCRINE-ENZYMATIC

Familial lymphocytic thyroiditis resulting in **hypothyroidism** has been reported Great Danes [13] The Orthopedic Foundation for animals (OFA) states that 5.5% of the Thyroid panels submitted to its registry were abnormal. [20] The breed is believed to be at an increased risk for **hypoadrenocorticism** (Addison's disease). [12(515), 13]

GASTROINTESTINAL

Great Danes are reported to be predisposed for **gingival hyperplasia**. [13]

A familial predisposition for **megaesophagus-esophageal hypomotility** has been reported in the Great Dane. [12(479) 13]

Gastric dilatation-volvulus (GDV) is the number one killer of Great Danes. [2, 13, 15] There is a 43 times greater risk of a Great Dane having GDV than the general population. [19] Multiple small meals and restricted exercise before and after meals may reduce the risk of GDV. It has been suggested that a prophylactic gastropexy be performed at the time of sterilization.

The Great Dane is overrepresented in the incidence of **splenomegaly** due either to **splenic torsion** or **hemangiosarcoma of the spleen**. [13]

DENTITION

Permanent teething starts at about 4 months. A scissors bite is correct. Any variance such as wry or missing teeth, overshot and undershot bites should be watched for. On a young developing mouth, a tight or even bite may go undershot (a serious fault). Often, the slightly overshot bite is more apt to develop into the correct scissors bite. Teething may have an effect on ear training because of the extra calcium drain on the animal's system. **Brachygnathism** (undershot jaw), **Prognathism** (overshot jaw), **Oligodontia** (missing teeth) and **wry mouth** (undershot or overshot jaw that affects only one half of the mouth) have all been recognized in Great Danes. [12]

MUSCULOSKELETAL

Hypertrophic osteodystrophy (HOD) [16c] and **panosteitis** [15] are two skeletal disorders seen in growing Great Danes. HOD is the more severe of the two conditions. Symptoms include acute lameness, lethargy, and a high fever. There is usually a firm, painful swelling at the level of the distal metaphyses of the radius and ulna.

Hip and **elbow dysplasia** [3] (**Ununited anconeal process**) occur in the breed. The Orthopedic Foundation for Animals lists the Great Dane as 84th in hip dysplasia with 12.0% abnormal and 58th in elbow dysplasia with 3.9% abnormal. [20] Lateral **patellar luxation** has been reported in Great Danes. [12(1101)]

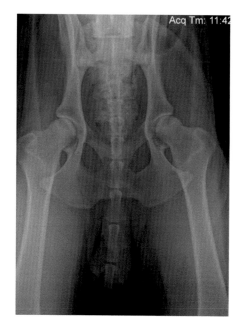 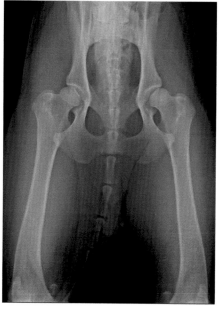

Normal Hips in a Great Dane   Moderate Hip Dysplasia Source:OFA

Osteochondrosis is the disturbance of endochondral ossification resulting in the excessive retention of cartilage over a joint surface with necrosis of the underlying bone. The condition causes different lesions in different breeds. In the Great Dane, **osteochondritis of the stifle** [12 (417)] [16c] and **antebrachial growth deformities** have been reported. [13]

Craniomandibular osteopathy a proliferative bone disease that affects the mandible, tympanic bullae and occasionally other bones in the head has been reported in the great Dane [12(1096)]

Diffuse idiopathic skeletal hyperostosis is a rare disorder reported in the Great Dane. The condition is similar to Forrestier's disease in man and features new bone formation along the vertebral bodies and hyperostosis of soft tissue such as ligaments, joints, tendons and muscles. [31]

Great Danes like other giant breeds are predisposed to **Osteosarcoma and hemangiosarcoma of the bone.** [13]

Myotonia is a condition of skeletal muscle characterized by sustained contraction that can occur in Great Danes. [21] The signs include a progressive stiffening of the gait with exercise. Diagnosis is obtained with electromyography.

Inherited Myopathy is a non-inflammatory muscle disease seen in young Great Danes. The condition has previously been referred to as central core Myopathy but is histologically different from that disease. Clinical signs include exercise intolerance, exercise induced tremors and muscle wasting. Onset usually occurs before one year of age and both males and females are equally affected. Elevated creatinine kinase levels have been reported. All reported cases have occured in fawn and brindle Danes. The disease is inherited as an autosomal recessive trait with a splicing mutation of the BIN1 gene being the cause. Paw Prints Genetics and the UC Davis Veterinary Genetics Lab offer a DNA test for inherited myopathy. [28, 37]

NEUROLOGICAL

Congenital deafness [11, 13] and **calcinosis circumscripta** [16d] are both know to occur in Great Danes.

Cervical vertebral instability [2, 5, 6] is the most significant neurological problem in the Great Dane. Unlike the Doberman Pinscher, this condition most often affects Great Danes between 6 months and 3 years of age and is the result of spinal cord compression due to cervical vertebral malformation. The lesions most often seen are dorsoventral compression of the vertebral foramina and malformation of the articular facets with the lesions occurring at C5, C6 and C7. This compression leads to a progressive ataxia and paresis of the rear limbs. [21]

Diskospondylitis is an infection of the vertebral column affecting the cartilaginous vertebral endplates with secondary involvement of the disks. Staphylococcus aureus is the most frequently reported infectious agent. It is spread via the blood from other locations such as abscesses and oral infections. Clinical signs are non-specific early on and include a malaise, anorexia and vertebral pain. Vertebral instability, luxation and neurologic deficits may occur later. A recent study indicated that the Great Dane was at 7.3 time's greater risk for diskospondylitis than the general population. [24]

A **cerebellar abiotrophy** [21] causing progressive cerebellar ataxia, tremors and dysmetria has been reported in the Great Dane and **Stockard's paralysis** [16d], a degenerative disease resulting in atrophy of the pelvic limbs was reported in Great Dane crosses.

OPHTHALMIC

Distichiasis: Note the presence of eyelashes directed toward the cornea

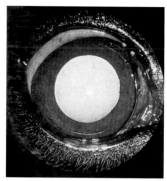

Cataract

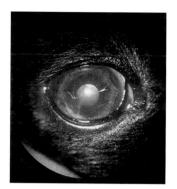

Persistent Pupillary Membranes

Microphthalmia [9, 10, 23] has been associated with partial albinism in the Great Dane. This condition appears to be linked with deafness in the breed. Harlequins would be the most often affected due to their color pattern. Multiple ocular defects of the iris, lens and retina are associated with the condition and are believed to be part of a common developmental defect. The disorder is believed to be inherited as an autosomal dominant trait.

Eury/Macroblepheron is an abnormally large palpebral fissure which can result in lower lid ectropion or upper lid entropion. [23]

Distichiasis, [23] **entropion,** [23] **ectropion** [23] and **eversion of the cartilage of the third eyelid** [7] are eyelid abnormalities found in the Great Dane.

Uveal hypopigmentation [8, 12(827)] is seen in the harlequin Great Dane and has been associated with deafness. It is one of the abnormalities seen with microphthalmia and has the same mode of inheritance. **Iris cysts** have also been reported in the breed. These sacs attach to the posterior surface of the iris and may break free and float into the anterior chamber.

Persistent pupillary membranes (PPM) have been recognized in Great Danes. [23] PPM are vascular remnants that have failed to regress existing in the anterior chamber of the eye. They may form bridges from the iris to the iris, the iris to the lens or cornea or form sheets in the anterior chamber. The number and location determine if they can cause vision impairment. Iris to iris PPM have been reported in Great Danes.

Ciliary body cysts [23] are cysts of pigmented tissue arising from the ciliary body. They remain attached or break free and float into the anterior chamber. In the Great Dane, these cysts may predispose the dog to **glaucoma.** [12 (110) 23]

Cataracts [12 (903) 23] are found in this breed and must be considered hereditary until proven otherwise.

Hemeralopia [12(1119)] is an inherited disease reported in the Great Dane. This is a progressive degeneration of the cones beginning at 6 weeks of age causing blindness in bright light.

Retinal dysplasia (folds and geographic) [12(1119)] has been associated with harlequin Great Danes.

Early onset **progressive retinal atrophy (PRA)** [12(903), 23] has been recognized in the Great Dane.

UROGENITAL

Cystinuria[12] has been reported anecdotally in the breed.

BEHAVIOR

Great Danes are steady, patient and affectionate. Good with children in the family, they can be reserved with strangers. Surveys conducted in Japan, Germany and the USA characterizes the Dane as a breed with low levels of activity and affection and reduced levels of playfulness. They have moderate tendencies toward territorial aggression and owner dominance as well as being somewhat destructive. They are considered above average in trainability. [33, 34, 35, 36]

Georgia......Owned by Jennifer Beard .....Photo by: Laurie Morris Witt

OLD AGE

The average life span of the Great Dane is a short 5 to 8 years. Older Danes hold their weight on little food and are generally easy keepers. Often small black growths (like moles) appear anywhere on the body and are best left alone unless they are growing rapidly or draining. Some degree of arthritis is most common in older Danes. A thick 2 to 4 inch soft, warm draft free bed is needed for comfort as well as for avoiding calluses that can become sore or develop into a lick granuloma or related problems. The most common causes of death are trauma, kidney failure, bloat and assorted forms of spinal degeneration. A survey of the Veterinary Medical Database lists gastrointestinal problems and cancer as the most commonly diagnosed causes of death in Great Danes. [29] This agrees with a survey conducted by the Great Dane Club of America which lists cancer, heart disease and bloat as the three most common causes of death. [30]

MISCELLANEOUS

Great Danes are predisposed for **hemangiosarcoma**[13] of the bone, spleen and liver.

MISCELLANEOUS FACTS & RESOURCES

This is a list of Genetic tests available for Great Danes to identify inherited medical problems that may be recommended by your Veterinarian

Condition: Laboratory
Merle Pattern: Vita Tech (IDEXX Canada)
Harlequin Pattern: UC Davis Vet Genetics Lab
Inherited Myopathy: UC Davis Vet Genetics Lab., Paw Prints Genetics

For information about the laboratories performing these tests and sample submission contact: www.offa.org/dna_labs.html

Additional health screening tests recommended for Great Danes by the Canine Health Information Center (CHIC)

Here is how CHIC works to help dog fanciers to improve their breeds

CHIC works with national breed clubs, the AKC Canine Health Foundation and the Orthopedic Foundation for Animals (OFA) to create a list of health screening procedures designed to eliminate inherited health problems from dogs used for breeding. The procedures vary from breed to breed and may change if new problems are identified or new tests become available. A dog must have completed all the required health screening procedures in order to receive a CHIC number. For more information contact: www.caninehealthinfo.org/

CHIC REQUIREMENTS FOR GREAT DANES

Hip Dysplasia: OFA, PennHip or OVC evaluation
Eye Exam by a boarded ACVO Ophthalmologist: Results registered with CERF or OFA
Autoimmune Thyroiditis: OFA evaluation from an approved laboratory
Congenital Cardiac Database: ARCH – ACVIM Registry of Cardiac Health or OFA evaluation [27]

NATIONAL BREED CLUB

The National Breed Club is a good place to discover all the things you can do with your Great Dane and to contact other Great Dane owners.

GREAT DANE CLUB OF AMERICA, INC.

www.gdca.org

REFERENCES

1. American Kennel Club, *Complete Dog Book*. (Howell Book House, New York, NY. 18th ed.1992) 262-266.
2. Trotter, E.J., deLahunta, A., Geary, J.C. and Brasmer, T.H. "Caudal Cervical Vertebrae Malformation-Malarticulation in Great Danes and Doberman Pinschers," *JAVMA*; 1976: 168(10): 917-930.
3. "Veterinary News," *American Kennel Club Gazette*; June, 1990.
4. Griffin, C., Kwochka, K., McDonald, *J. Current Veterinary Dermatology, the Science and Art of Therapy*. Mosby Yearbook, St. Louis, MO. 1993: 171,266.
5. Ettinger, S.J.: Textbook of Veterinary Medicine. W.B. Saunders, Co., Philadelphia, PA 1989: 640.
6. Conrad, C. Radiology Section. Purdue University, W. Lafayette, IN., Personal Communication. 1975.
7. Magrane, W.G. *Canine Ophthalmology*. (Lea & Febiger, Philadelphia, PA., l968) 232.
8. Kirk, R.W. *Current Veterinary Therapy VI*. (W.B. Saunders, Philadelphia, PA. 1977) 73.
9. *Canine Practice*. 4(4): 60 August, 1977.
10. Mitchel, A.L. "Dominant Dilution and Other Color Factors in Collie Dogs," *J. Hered.*; 1935: 26: 424-430.
11. Strain, George M. "Deafness in Dogs and Cats," *Proc. 10th Forum*; May, 1992.
12. Ackerman, Lowell, The Genetic Connection: A Guide to Health Problems in Purebred Dogs. Lakewood, CO; AAHA Press. 1999
13. Tilley, Lawrence P., smith, Francis W.K. Jr. The 5 Minute Consult; Canine and Feline 4th ed. Ames, IA, Blackwell Publishing 2007
14. Kittleson Mark, D., Kienle, Richard D. Small Animal Cardiovascular Medicine. St. Louis, MO; Mosby Inc. 1998
15. Great Dane Club of America Inc. website: www.gdca.org Health and Welfare section.
    a. Harlequin and Merle Research News, Health and Welfare section.
16. a. Moise, N. Sidney, Tricuspid valve dysplasia in the dog. P. 813
    b. Power, Helen T., Ihrke, Peter J. The use of synthetic retinoids in veterinary medicine. P. 585
    c. Schrader, Steven C. Differential diagnosis of nontraumatic causes of lameness in young growing dogs. P. 1171
    d. Coates, Joan R., Kline, Karen L. Congenital and inherited neurologic disorders in dogs and cats. P. 1111 Kirk's Current Veterinary Therapy XII. Philadelphia, PA; W.B. Saunders Co. 1995
17. Meurs, Kathryn M., Miller, Mathew W., Wright, Nicola A. Clinical features of dilated cardiomyopathy in Great Danes and results of a pedigree analysis: 17 cases (1990-2000) JAVMA, Vol. 218, No. 5, March 1, 2001
18. Scott, Danny W. , Miller, William H. Jr. Griffin, Craig E. Muller and Kirk's Small Animal Dermatology-6th ed. Philadelphia, PA; W.B. Saunders Co. 2001
19. Dorn, Richard Canine breed specific risks of frequently diagnosed diseases at Veterinary teaching hospitals. Raleigh, NC; AKC Canine Health Foundation
20. Orthopedic Foundation for Animals website: www.offa.org
21. Oliver, John E. Jr., Lorenz, Michael D. Korngay, Joe N. Handbook of Veterinary Neurology, 3rd ed. Philadelphia, PA W.B. Saunders Co. 1997
22. Targett, M.P., Franklin, R.J.M., Olby, N.J. et.al. Central core myopathy in a Great Dane. J Small Animal Practice 35: 100-103, 1994
23. Genetics Committee of the American College of Veterinary Ophthalmologists, Ocular Disorders Presumed to be Inherited in Purebred Dogs. 5th ed. 2009
24. Burkert, Blaine A., Kerwin, Sharon C., Hosgood, G.L. ET. al. Signalment and clinical features of diskospondylitis in dogs: 513 cases (1980-2001). JAVMA, Vol. 227, No. 2, July 15, 2005. p. 268-74
25. Clark, Leigh Anne, Wahl, J.M., Rees, C.A. and Murphy, K.E. ET. al. Retrotransposon insertion in SILV is responsible for merle patterning of the domestic dog. PNAS 2006; 0: 50694010 www.pnas.org/cgi/reprint/0506940103v1
26. GenMARK: www.genmarkag.com/home_companion.php
27. Great Dane Breed Requirements, Canine Health Information Center: www.caninehealthinfo.org

28. Lujan Feliu-Pasccual, A., Sheldon, G.D., Targett, M.P. ET AL, Inherited Myopathy in Great Danes. Journal of Small Animal Practice May 2006, 47(5) 249-54

29. Fleming, J.M., Creevy, K.E., Promislow, D.E.L. Mortality in North American Dogs from 1984 to 2004: an Investigation into Age-, Size-, and Breed-Related Causes of Death Journal of Veterinary Internal Medicine Vol. 25, Issue 2 March/April 2011 pages 187-198

30. Great Dane Club of America National Health Survey, 1-19-04: www.gdca.org/surveyfinal.pdf

31. Morgan, J.P., Stavenborn, M. Disseminated Idiopathic Skeletal Hyperostosis (DISH) in a Dog Vet. Radiology 32 ;(2): 65-70 March 1991

32. Clark, L.A., Tsai, K.L., Starr, A.N. ET AL A missense mutation in the 20S proteasome B2 subunit of Great Danes having harlequin coat patterning Genomics 2011 Apr; 97(4): 244-8

33. Hart, B.L., Hart, L. The Perfect Puppy, How to Choose Your Dog by Its Behavior New York, Barnes & Noble Books, 2001

34. Duffy, D.L., Yuying, H., Serpell, J. A. Breed differences in canine aggression Appl. Anim. Behav Sci (2008)

35. Takeuchi, Y. Mori, Y. A Comparison of the Behavioral Profiles of Purebred Dogs in Japan to Profiles of those in the United States and the United Kingdom J Vet Med Sci 68 789-90 2006

36. Turcsan, B., Kubinyi, E. Miklosi, A. Trainability and boldness traits differ between dog breed clusters based on conventional breed categories and genetic relatedness Appl Anim Behav Sci 2011 132:61-70